BH Ch.1
85-86

# ALONE

# alone

Richard A. Boning

*Illustrated by*

Harry Schaare

## The Incredible Series

Dexter & Westbrook, Ltd., Baldwin, New York

*To*

*Eldon E. Ekwall*

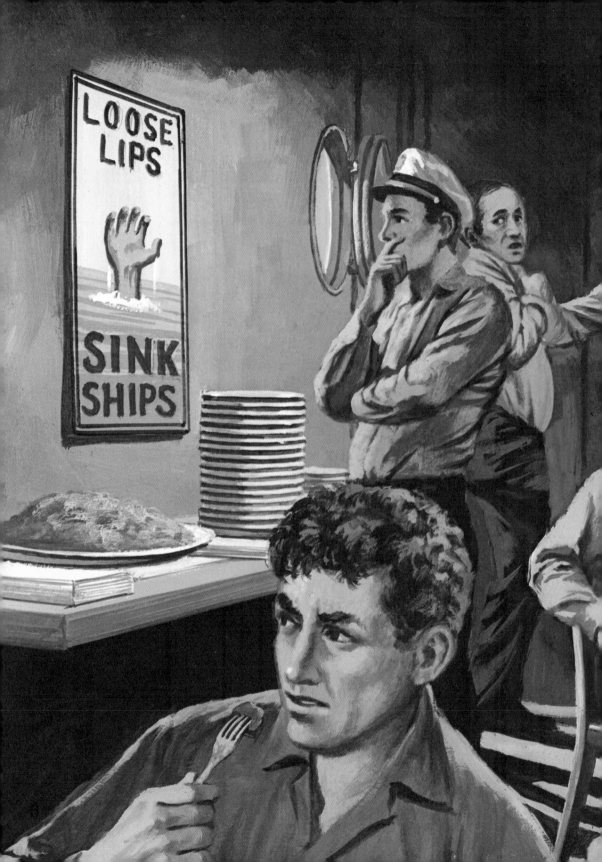

It was November, 1942—a month of terror aboard the *Benlomond*. British merchant ships were being sent to the bottom at an alarming rate, especially in these submarine-infested waters off Africa. The crew was tense. Fights broke out. Only Poon Lim, the little Chinese steward, was unafraid. He was far too busy with his duties to worry about German submarines.

While his mates wrangled, Poon quietly served lunch. In a few days they would reach Dutch Guiana. As Poon worked, he heard his mates boast of the liquor they would consume. Poon paid little heed. He might venture ashore for some good Chinese food. He would also buy gifts for his family. But that was all. Like his mates, he was unaware that the slow-moving *Benlomond* was now lined up in the sights of a German submarine.

As Poon set a dish on the table, the mess hall seemed to explode under his feet. For a moment he was stunned. Then he knew what had happened. Throughout the ship rang the shouts and sobs of terrified crew members. Poon wasted no time on idle yells. He raced out on deck. Quickly he strapped on a life jacket. There was no time to lose. The ship was sinking rapidly.

Taking a deep breath, Poon hurled his small frame out into the cold Atlantic. Quickly he swam away with the overhand stroke he had learned as a boy on the seacoast of China. In a few minutes he heard a muffled roar. The boilers had exploded. The *Benlomond* disappeared. Poon had leaped just in time.

As a wave lifted him high in the air, Poon sighted a raft. On it were four men struggling with oars. Poon yelled frantically, but the men did not hear him. Then he tried to swim in the direction of the raft, but it faded from sight. The little steward was now truly alone.

Poon had no time to consider his plight. It took all of his strength to keep from drowning. Despite his life jacket, large waves broke over his head. Sputtering and gagging, he tried to keep water out of his lungs. He was rapidly losing the battle when he sighted another raft ahead. This one was empty. Wearily, he swam to it. With his last strength, he pulled himself aboard. Thus began one of the greatest survival stories in history.

After resting for long minutes, Poon raised himself and searched the horizon. Where was the other raft? To his disappointment there was no sign of it. Then he brightened as he realized the sailors on the other raft could cover a larger area because of their oars. Their chances of being sighted by a boat or plane were excellent. The sinking would be reported and a search-and-rescue mission sent out for survivors.

But Poon did not know that the sailors on the other raft would never be heard from again. Of all fifty people on the *Benlomond*, he was the only survivor.

The young steward now found himself on an eight-foot raft — a mere dot in the middle of the vast Atlantic. The water below was a mile deep. To the north lay the Azores, to the East — Africa. But Poon was not drifting in either of these directions.

As he took stock, he found much to be thankful for. Under a canvas, he discovered tins of good British biscuit, a jug of water, a few matches, a flashlight, and some rockets. Not much, but enough to keep him alive for several weeks. Rescue would certainly come by then.

Poon carefully rationed his food and water and be-gan to search the horizon. Day after day he drifted. One week passed. Then another. By now Poon had given up hope of a search-and-rescue mission. Instead, he must stay alive until a vessel or a plane chanced upon him.

At the beginning of the fourth week his prayers were answered. A steamer sailed out of the horizon directly toward him. Poon rarely permitted himself emotion, but his heart leaped up. As the ship drew nearer, he saw that it was a merchant ship. It would pass very close.

He almost felt like laughing with relief. Instead, he raised the water jar. There was no need to ration water now. Or food either. He took a large swallow. Then he began eating biscuit hungrily. In a few minutes the ship would be upon him.

Then suddenly he knew shame. What of his manners? In honor of the occasion he lighted his rockets. They shot up into the sky in brilliant arcs. At the end of each arc, the rocket exploded with a gentle pop. As Poon fired each salute of welcome, he danced for joy.

Now the ship was almost directly opposite him. He could make out individual figures on the deck. Sailors pointed at him. Some climbed aloft where they could get a better view. Sunlight glinted on the binoculars of the lookout. Poon waved and shouted. But then he suddenly knew fear. Why wasn't the ship slowing down?

Anxiously he yelled, "Stop! It is I — Poon Lim!"

But the ship continued on by. The sailors on deck did not return his wave. They merely stared. In despair Poon let his arms drop. Why were they leaving him here?

Then he knew the answer. On occasion U-boats had placed a live decoy on a raft. When a merchant ship stopped to rescue the "survivor," the U-boat had blown the ship to bits. Evidently this merchant vessel feared that Poon was such a decoy.

In minutes the figures on the deck had become much smaller. In an hour the ship had sailed over the horizon. Soon all that was left was a smudge of smoke. Then this too was gone. The little steward had never known such loneliness.

Poon cut his rations even further and continued to search the horizon. Days passed. Weeks passed, and still the raft drifted toward an unknown destination. Then on the afternoon of the forty-fifth day Poon saw something that made him forget his hunger. Angry clouds of a tropical storm were forming in the south. If Poon did not think of some means of clinging to the raft, death would come swiftly.

Quickly he lashed down his provisions with one rope. With another he tied one hand to the end of a plank. With a third he tied his leg to one of the spikes that projected above the planks. Then he lay on the raft and waited. He knew that the awesome power heading toward him could sweep him off the raft like a cricket from a bamboo leaf.

First came the rain. It flayed him until he almost cried out in pain. The drops stung like pellets. Then the full force of the storm struck. One minute the raft seemed to hang in midair. The next it was sliding down a huge wave. Poon was raised from the raft and hurled down against the planks, leaving him gasping for breath. Would the ropes hold? A large wave picked up the raft and slammed his head down savagely. He knew no more.

Hours later Poon regained consciousness. The sea was calm, and the sun was beating down again. As he untied the ropes, his head spun. He knew that the storm must have been brief. But he could not count on such luck again. Even though his bones ached, he roused himself and searched the horizon eagerly. There was no sign of a ship.

Day followed day. Poon kept track of time by an old Chinese method — using the moon. But on the morning of the fiftieth day, although he had been able to catch rain water with the canvas, he was down to his last two biscuits. His ribs stuck out. Unless something happened soon, he would starve.

As he considered his fate, Poon heard a faint hum. It sounded like a mosquito. Swiftly he scanned the sky. Then he saw it! A plane — flying low and directly toward him.

In a moment he could make out the plane's insignia. It was an American fighter plane. Poon jumped up and down and shouted. The plane banked directly overhead. It began to circle the raft. Poon was wild with joy.

As the plane flew over him, Poon could see the pilot looking down. Poon rubbed his stomach. There was no way to mistake this sign of hunger! Would the pilot drop any food? Twice the plane circled. But to Poon's dismay nothing was dropped.

As Poon watched with dwindling hope, the plane flew east and disappeared in the rays of the sun. Once again the sound of the engine became the whine of a mosquito. Then even the whine was gone, and Poon heard only the slap of the waves against the raft. Once more he was alone.

Poon's body was weak, but his mind was strong and clear as it wrestled with the problem of survival. The little steward realized that he could no longer depend on any one else for help. If he were to survive, he must rely on himself. Somehow he must find a way to obtain food from the sea.

But how? Could he make a fishing line? Could he weave one from the strands of rope? Perhaps. A hook, however, was a different matter!

Poon studied his meager store of supplies. Only one object was made of metal — the flashlight. It was useless for his purpose. Or was it? Under the cap was a coiled wire. If he could remove this wire, he would have a fishhook. He tried for hours, but the wire would not budge.

Poon looked around the raft thoughtfully. The head of a projecting spike caught his gaze and gave him an idea. For two days Poon gnawed at the spike with his teeth. Finally it lay in his hand. He quickly pried the wire out of the flashlight. Now he had his hook!

Baiting the hook with a piece of his last biscuit, Poon lowered it into the dark depths below. He had fished many times for enjoyment. This time he must fish for his life! To his disappointment, the tough British biscuit quickly dissolved in the water. The bare hook glittered mockingly.

Poon pondered this new problem. Unless he could soon catch fish, he would die. He was skin and bones now. But where could he find bait tough enough to stay on the hook? Then he realized that he had been at sea long enough for barnacles to form beneath the raft. He reached under the edge and pulled one up joyfully. Baiting the hook, he once again lowered his line.

In an hour his patience was rewarded. Elated, Poon pulled a fish from the water. It was small, but it gleamed in the sunlight like a jewel. For a moment hunger tempted Poon. He could almost taste the cool, sweet flesh of the fish. But he knew it would be only a mouthful. He must use this small fish to capture a larger one. He must also use a larger hook. This was provided by the spike, which he hammered into the shape of a hook with his water jug. Poon placed the large hook through the tail of the small fish. Then he braided extra strands to his line. It must be strong. Gently he placed the fish in the water. It swam away, down into the depths, trailing the line behind it.

Poon waited. The line twitched feebly as the small fish swam below the raft. Then the movement stopped. Had his bait escaped? Suddenly the line hissed! Poon managed to wrap it around his hand to prevent it from slipping away. Even though he braced himself against the raft with his feet, he was almost pulled into the water. As the line made sharp, zigzag motions, he knew he had hooked a monster! Would he be strong enough to haul it onto the raft?

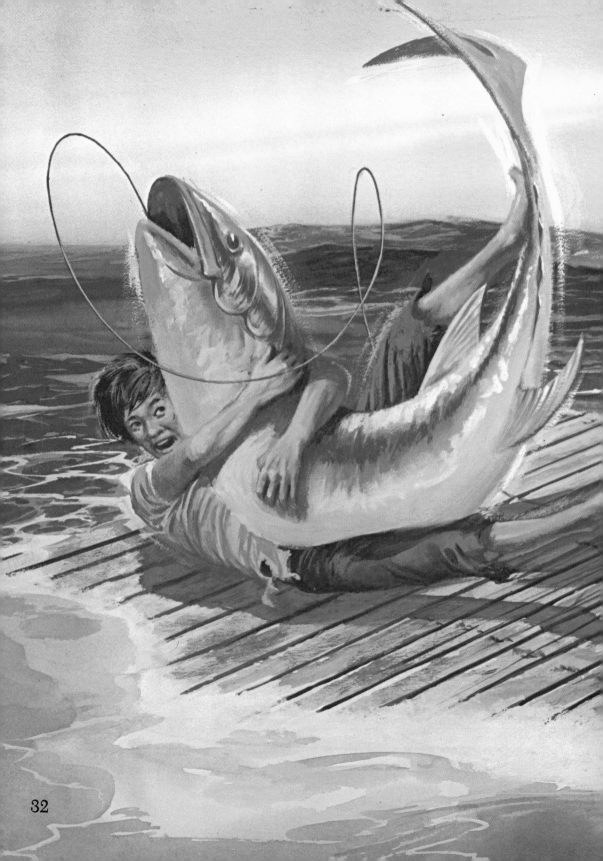

When the fish finally broke water, Poon was astounded. It was larger than Poon himself! Somehow he managed to get it aboard the raft. The fish flailed wildly about. Unless he acted quickly, he would lose his prize.

Poon struggled to hold the thrashing fish. Skillfully, he tore the large hook from its mouth. Using all his strength, he struck with the hook again and again. Finally the point lodged in the brain of the mighty fish. It shivered and lay still.

Eagerly Poon used a piece of the biscuit tin to hack chunks from the flanks of the fish. He crammed one into his mouth. He had eaten many fine, raw fish as a boy in Hainan. But never had he tasted a fish as delicious as this! The cool juices ran down his throat. If only he had some rice cakes, he would have a feast!

Day followed day. One morning Poon realized it was Christmas. On board the *Benlomond* there would be gifts. The cook would make a huge plum pudding. But with sadness Poon realized that there was no *Benlomond*.

For weeks Poon caught fish of all types. Then, during the middle of January, he made a frightening discovery. No matter how hard he tried, the fish refused to bite! This part of the ocean seemed suddenly barren.

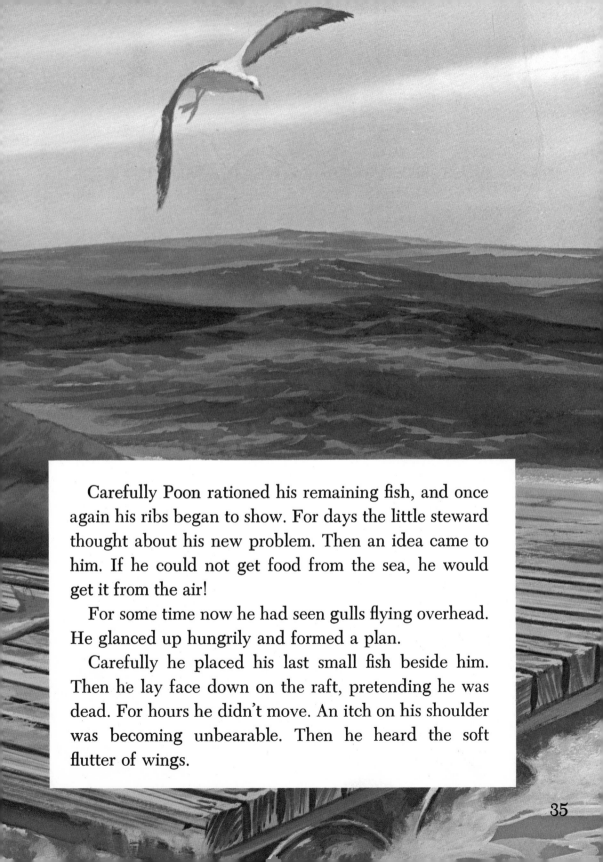

Carefully Poon rationed his remaining fish, and once again his ribs began to show. For days the little steward thought about his new problem. Then an idea came to him. If he could not get food from the sea, he would get it from the air!

For some time now he had seen gulls flying overhead. He glanced up hungrily and formed a plan.

Carefully he placed his last small fish beside him. Then he lay face down on the raft, pretending he was dead. For hours he didn't move. An itch on his shoulder was becoming unbearable. Then he heard the soft flutter of wings.

Slowly Poon opened his eyes. He found himself looking squarely into the eyes of a gull that stood only two feet away. A glint of understanding shone in the bird's eyes. Poon knew he must act fast or it would be too late.

The gull spread its wings and was already in the air when Poon lunged and seized it by the neck. The bird struggled frantically, ripping at Poon's chest. Heavy wings beat against his arms. It was a fight for survival in which there could be only one winner. Although he was weak from lack of food, Poon slowly forced the bird to the raft. As it squawked and screeched, he hammered its head against the planks. Finally it lay still.

For a long time Poon sat gasping beside the dead bird. His chest heaved. With his piece of biscuit tin he cut the bird into sections. It was tough and oily. But it was meat. Poon could feel the strength returning to his body.

On the morning of his 125th day at sea Poon received the strangest visitor of all.

He heard a loud gurgling noise behind him. Turning, he saw a submarine rising from the black depths! It floated to the surface just fifty yards away, water bubbling around its hull! On the conning tower was the swastika of the Nazi enemy! The hatch cover opened, and a team of German sailors raced to the forward gun. They went through a gun drill under the eyes of their officers.

No one looked in Poon's direction. But he knew that they had seen him.

An officer barked a command, and the crew pointed the gun at a sea gull swimming on the surface two hundred yards away. Another order: *"Laden! Fertig! Feuer!"* "Load! Ready! Fire!" The gun roared, and the sea gull disappeared in a geyser of water.

Now the Germans turned toward Poon. He looked back stoically. The crew swiveled the gun toward him. The two officers talked to each other for a moment, and Poon knew they were discussing his fate. Would they kill him? He stared at them without emotion. Then one of the officers barked a command. The crew trotted back to the conning tower. The hatch closed with a clang. In a moment water bubbled around the submarine again as it disappeared from sight. Once more Poon was alone.

On the 130th day Poon noticed that there was something different about the water. What was it? Then he
realized that it was no longer the deep indigo blue of
mid-ocean. Instead, it was a lighter hue.

The next day he saw an empty tin can in the water.
That afternoon a flock of land birds flew over the raft.

On the morning of the 133rd day he saw a sight that made him rub his eyes in disbelief. On the horizon lay a small sailboat. Land must be nearby! He began to yell and wave. Poon realized that he might not be seen or heard, but he knew that this time he *must* not fail. To the south thunderheads were building up. He would not get another chance.

Slowly the boat drew closer. In an hour he could see that there were four men aboard. Poon jumped up and down. Somehow he *must* make them see him!

"It is I — Poon Lim!" he shouted.

Long moments passed. Then one of the men gestured, and the boat began to sail directly toward him. They stared in astonishment. Minutes later they were alongside. As they examined Poon, his raft, and his equipment, they began to jabber at each other in a strange tongue.

They must be Spanish. *"De donde viene?"* Poon asked. "Where do you come from?" But they did not seem to understand. Instead they talked among themselves in a language he had never heard. Poon tried again.

*"Hablan portugues?"* "Do you speak Portuguese?"

Mouths flashed handsome white teeth. *"Sim, portugues."* "Yes, Portuguese," they said. Then they clapped him on the back, and everyone laughed with pleasure. But Poon wondered how he could have drifted to Portugal. Impossible! He must be near the Azores. *"Azores?"* he inquired.

*"Nao,"* "No," said one of them.

Pointing back over the horizon, he uttered a word that filled Poon with wonder. *"Brasil,"* he said.

When he realized the distance he had come, Poon's mind reeled. Without help from anyone, using tools he had fashioned himself, he had made one of the most incredible sea journeys in history. He had drifted 1200 miles from mid-ocean to the coast of Brazil on a raft no bigger than a tabletop. It would be a tale told for centuries — and a tale that Poon would someday tell his grandchildren.

But right now he wanted to savor this moment as he had no other. He did not speak the language of these men. But they understood him — and he them. No words were necessary.

The ordeal of Poon Lim was over. He was no longer alone.